The Hermitage in 1 Hour

State Rooms

Masterpieces

of Western European Painting:

14th — 18th Centuries

St Petersburg
ARCA
2013

Francesco Bartolomeo Rastrelli
The Winter Palace
View from Palace Square

The State Hermitage
is among the European museums that
are housed in palatial residences, like
the Louvre in Paris, the Palazzo Pitti in
Florence or the Vatican Palace in Rome.
In 1752, on the orders of Empress
Elizabeth, the architect Francesco
Bartolomeo Rastrelli began work on a
new imperial residence in St Petersburg.
It was practically finished when the
Empress died on Christmas Day 1761.
After a brief time as master of the
new palace, in June 1762 Peter III was
deposed in a coup and his wife took the
throne as Catherine II. In her apartments
in the Winter Palace the new empress
of Russia created a private museum that
she called the Hermitage. Today the
name is used for the whole huge complex
that grew from the Winter Palace. In the
1760s it was four or five rooms. Paintings
were hung in one; another was used

to display articles made of precious materials; the rest contained works of Chinese applied art.

The Old Hermitage (originally known as the Large Hermitage) extended as far as the Winter Canal and was connected by an arch to the Theatre constructed by the architect Giacomo Quarenghi.

The starting date for the Hermitage collection is customarily taken to be 1764. A combination of collecting passion and political calculation enabled Catherine the Great and Alexander I to put together one of the finest collections in Europe.

In the following reign, under Nicholas I, the Hermitage became a public museum. That took place in the middle of the nineteenth century. But before that, in late 1837 tragedy struck: the Winter Palace was gutted by fire and took two years to restore.

After that the Tsar invited the Bavarian architect Leo von Klenze to design the New Hermitage. Klenze succeeded in creating a worthy home for the masterpieces, whose number Nicholas also increased. The Russian sculptor Alexander Terebenev very impressively embellished the new western portico of the museum with huge atlantes carved from Serdobol granite.

The museum was opened on 5 February 1852. Nicholas strolled around the rooms with great satisfaction, saying, "Yes, it really is beautiful!"

Today it is hard to call the Hermitage simply a museum. It is more of an immense cultural and research centre. Over almost two and a half centuries one of the world's largest collections has been assembled here, numbering around three million works of art and artefacts of world culture, from the Stone Age up to the present century.

WE BEGIN OUR WALK AROUND THE MUSEUM with the Main Staircase that we reach by way of a spacious gallery containing vases and sculpture.

The Main or Jordan Staircase
Francesco Bartolomeo Rastrelli,
1754–62
Restored after the 1837 fire by Vasily
Stasov

In the eighteenth century this was known as the Ambassadors' Staircase as foreign delegations and guests would ascend it for an audience with the Russian monarch. In the nineteenth century it became known as the Jordan Staircase: at the Orthodox Feast of the Epiphany or the Baptism of Christ the imperial family descended by it to the Neva, which in the symbolic Blessing of the Waters ceremony represented the biblical Jordan. After the 1837 fire Vasily Stasov restored the main staircase, seeking to preserve Rastrelli's Baroque treatment of space.

In keeping with the architect's concept, the beauty of the staircase reveals itself in stages as you ascend. Going up the stairs, flanked by a balustrade of white Carrara marble, visitors reach the landing where the stairs split into two flights, and are forced to turn and admire the glorious view.

Some of the statues that stand in niches were brought here from the Summer Garden and Taurida Palace. Mirrors reflecting the daylight and the glitter of gold create a sense of festiveness and space. Overhead is the huge Baroque ceiling painting depicting Mount Olympus (by the eighteenth-century Venetian artist Gasparo Tiziani). The composition is completed by ten monolithic columns of grey Serdobol granite that support the vaults of the ceiling.

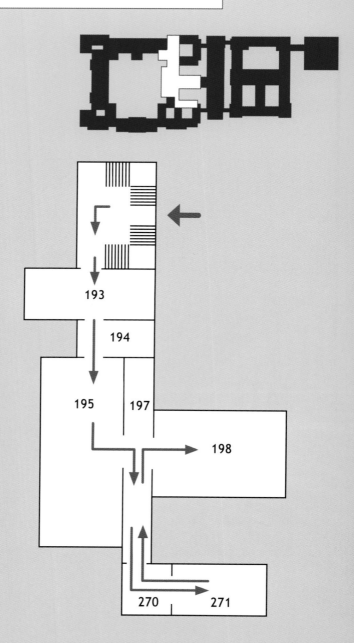

193

194

195 197

198

270 271

Beyond the Main Staircase the grand halls of the Winter Palace begin – the Great Enfilade of State Rooms.
On the upper landing of the Main Staircase we turn left and pass into the Field Marshals' Hall (Hall 193).

The Field Marshals' Hall
Auguste Montferrand, 1833-34
Restored after the 1837 fire
by Vasily Stasov
■ Hall 193

In contrast to the opulent Main Staircase the Field Marshals' Hall is plain and straightforward, something characteristic of Neo-Classicism in architecture. The walls, pilasters and columns are faced with white artificial marble. The hall obtains its festive grandeur from a multicoloured parquet floor, murals and bas-reliefs with a military theme and three gilded bronze chandeliers.

Montferrand created the Field Marshals' Hall in 1833 in place of three rooms designed by Rastrelli and after the fire Stasov restored it without any major changes. The hall got its name from the portraits of Russian field marshals hung between the pilasters.

Beyond the Field Marshals' Hall comes the Hall of Peter the Great or Small Throne Room (Hall 194).

The Hall of Peter the Great (Small Throne Room)
Auguste Montferrand, 1833
Restored after the 1837 fire by Vasily Stasov
■ Hall 194

For all the austerity of its architectural forms, the hall is luxuriously finished. The walls are lined with Lyons velvet embroidered with silver. The vaulted ceiling is embellished with golden Russian coats-of-arms executed in a unique technique of extremely fine hatching. The parquet floor is made of precious varieties of wood. Peter's monogram (two Latin P's), the double-headed eagle, crown and naval motifs all remind the visitor of the first Russian emperor's time.

The niche in the form of a triumphal arch contains a throne of bog oak and gilded silver made by the English craftsman Nicholas Clausen. Above the throne, between two solid jasper columns is Jacopo Amiconi's depiction of Peter the Great beside Minerva, the goddess of wisdom.

From the relatively small Hall of Peter the Great we emerge into the resplendent Armorial Hall (Hall 195).

The Armorial Hall
Vasily Stasov, 1838-39
Hall 195

The present interior of the Armorial Hall was created in the mid-nineteenth century. In Rastrelli's time this was the location of the Bright Gallery that was reconstructed in the late 1700s by the architect Yury Velten. After the fire Stasov enlarged Velten's hall and altered certain details.

This grand columned hall with a floor area of about 1,000 square metres, was intended for magnificent balls and receptions. The fluted Corinthian columns, ornaments of the frieze, balustrade and military trophies above the upper tier of windows are all gilded.

Standing by the end walls are sculptural groups of Russian warriors with banners and heraldic symbols. The coats-of-arms of the Russian provinces are depicted on shields attached to the gilded bronze chandeliers.

Taking the door on the left in the Armorial Hall we find ourselves in one of the most famous galleries in the museum - the Gallery of 1812 (Hall 197).

The Gallery of 1812
Carlo Rossi, 1826
Restored after the 1837 fire
by Vasily Stasov
■ Hall 197

This gallery was created as a memorial to Russia's triumph in the "Patriotic War" of 1812. After the 1837 fire it was restored in its original form to Rossi's design.

The walls are hung with 332 portraits of participants in the titanic struggle against Napoleon. They were painted over some ten years by George Dawe, an English artist invited to Russia by Alexander I, and his Russian assistants Alexander Poliakov and Vasily (Wilhelm) Golicke. The rows of chest-length depictions are interrupted by full-length portraits of the commanders-in-chief of the Russian and allied armies.

Two of them show Field Marshals Kutuzov and Barclay de Tolly.

At the end of the gallery are formal portraits of Alexander I and two monarchs who joined him in the fight against Napoleon – King Frederick William of Prussia and Emperor Francis I of Austria.

The majority of the portraits were painted from life. Thirteen empty frames have been left filled with green cloth in memory of men whose appearance was unknown as they died without leaving any likeness of themselves.

Opposite the portrait of Alexander I is the entrance to the Winter Palace church (Halls 270-271) that linked the state rooms and living apartments.

The Great Church of the Winter Palace
Francesco Bartolomeo Rastrelli, 1754-62
Restored after the 1837 fire
by Vasily Stasov
▨ Hall 270-271

The church was one of Rastrelli's last
creations in the Winter Palace, shortly
before his dismissal. Festive church
services were an inseparable part of all
official ceremonies in the Russian Empire
and so Rastrelli placed the Great Church
alongside the suite of state rooms and
connected it to the private apartments of
Catherine II. From here, after receiving
communion, the Empress went off "to
serve the country".

After the 1837 fire Vasily Stasov
restored the church in its former
appearance, assisted by the artists Piotr
Basin and Fiodor Bruni who recreated
the depictions of the four Evangelists
below the dome and the ceiling painting
of the Resurrection that were originally
painted by the Italian artist Francesco
Fontebasso.

**We return to the Gallery of 1812
(Hall 197) and enter the St George Hall
or Large Throne Room (Hall 198).**

The St George Hall (Large Throne Room)
Giacomo Quarenghi, 1795
Restored after the 1837 fire by Vasily
Stasov and Nikolai Yefimov, 1842
▨ Hall 198

On 26 November 1795, the Orthodox
feast of St George, the patron saint
of Russia, the new Throne Room that
Quarenghi had created for the Winter
Palace was formally inaugurated. After
the 1837 fire Stasov and Yefimov retained
the original compositional approach when
they restored the hall.

The St George Hall, with a floor
area of about 800 square metres, was
used for official receptions and grand
ceremonies. The hall is justly considered
a masterpiece of Russian nineteenth-
century Neo-Classical architecture. The
architects succeeded in giving classic
proportions to a sumptuous gala interior.
The pattern of the parquet floor, made
from rare varieties of wood, repeats the
ceiling décor.

The throne was created in 1731-32
to a commission from Empress Anna
Ioannovna.

The St George Hall is interesting
not only for its decoration, but also
for its structural properties: instead of
a traditional wooden superstructure,
Stasov employed for the first time here
an innovative metal construction that
supports a ceiling of copper sheets.

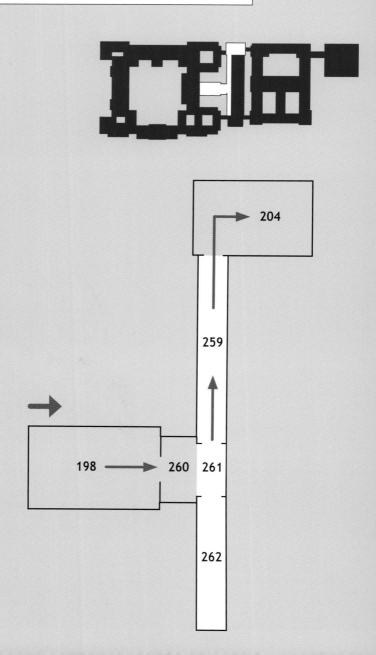

NETHERLANDISH PAINTING
of the 15th and 16th centuries

FIRST
FLOOR

204

259

198 → 260 261

262

Through the adjoining room (Hall 260) we enter the Western Gallery of the Small Hermitage (Halls 262, 261 and 259) and turn to the left. Medieval applied art and the Netherlandish painting of the 15th and 16th centuries are displayed in the Gallery.

This small two-part altarpiece was created in the period when Netherlandish painting was emerging and flourishing. In it we can detect all the conventionality of the art of the previous era as well as new figurative devices.

The traditional approach is especially evident in the Trinity (the left-hand panel of the diptych), where the image is arranged in keeping with the icon-painting tradition.

Robert Campin
The Holy Trinity
Virgin and Child by a Fireplace
Diptych. 1430s
Oil on panel
34.3 × 24.5 cm (each section)
█ Hall 261

The body of the dead Christ in the arms of God the Father with a dove symbolizing the Holy Spirit perched on Christ's shoulder. Echoes of the Gothic tradition can be detected in the contours of the rigid figures, in the manner of depicting the drapes and in the very character of the composition.

The right-hand panel is less conservative. The artist experimented boldly with the construction of a three-dimensional space and strove to give objects volume through the use of light-and-shade modelling. But, most significantly, the Virgin and Child by a Fireplace comes across as

more of a genre painting than an icon. Campin depicted Mary in the guise of a simple Low Countries townswoman in the interior of a contemporary burgher home. She is lovingly swaddling her child and, as if fearing to disturb the infant with a cold touch, warms her hand by the fire. Elements of everyday life are intertwined in the painting with Christian symbolism: the towel and washstand represent Mary's purity; the soft light flooding the room indicates a spiritual dimension.

Both compositions were executed in the oil-painting technique introduced by Campin's famous contemporary Jan van Eyck. The works are marked by an exceptionally beautiful palette and glowing paints.

The diptych came into the Hermitage in 1845 from the collection of Dmitry Tatishchev.

Rogier van der Weyden
St Luke Painting the Virgin
1430s
Oil on canvas, transferred from panel
102.5 × 108.5 cm
▨ Hall 261

The subject of this painting derives from a Greek legend that Luke was the first to make a depiction of the Virgin Mary. It has been suggested that Rogier gave Luke his own facial features.

Mary sits in an open loggia at the foot of a throne suckling the infant Christ. The painting is full of Christian symbolism: the throne reminds us of the Kingdom of Heaven, the figures of Adam and Eve of Original Sin that the Saviour redeemed. Behind the apostle's back we can see a bull and a book – his traditional attributes.

The Low Countries city with an almost fairy-tale appearance is being contemplated by a couple that are possibly Mary's parents, Joachim and Anne.

This painting came into the Hermitage in two separate parts: St Luke in 1850, following the sale of the Dutch king William II's collection in the Hague, the Virgin and Child only in 1884.

We walk through the display of mediaeval applied art to the end of the Western Gallery and then turn right to reach the Pavilion Hall (Hall 204).

The Pavilion Hall of the Small Hermitage
Andrei Stakenschneider
1850s
Hall 204

Until the mid-nineteenth-century reconstruction the site of the Pavilion Hall was occupied by a Winter Garden. The architect Stakenschneider united the garden with the adjoining rooms to create a strikingly beautiful hall with two rows of windows that became known as the Pavilion Hall. The interior is a harmonious blend of Neo-Classical, Renaissance and Eastern architectural motifs. The mosaic of colour glass smaltos on the floor in the southern part of the hall is based on an ancient original. It was created in 1847-51 by craftsmen from the St Petersburg Academy of Arts copying mosaics in the baths of Emperor Titus in Rome. Thanks to the tall windows on all four sides the hall is transfused with light and air. The crystal drops of twenty-eight chandeliers glittering with coloured refractions and the gilded ornament create a special sense of festive grandeur.

The display in the hall includes a real masterpiece of applied art - the Peacock Clock made by the Englishman James Cox. When it strikes the hour the figures go into motion: the peacock spreads its tail, the owl turns its head and the cockerel crows. The time is shown by figures in the cap of a large mushroom. This fantastic timepiece was bought by Prince Potemkin in 1780.

ITALIAN PAINTING
of the 13th and 16th centuries

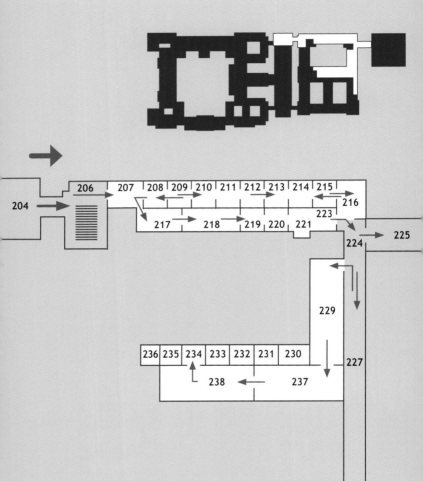

After leaving the Pavilion Hall (Hall 204) we continue our tour in the Old and New Hermitages, visiting masterpieces of Italian, Spanish, Flemish and Dutch art.

We are now on the upper landing of the Council Staircase (Hall 206) that was created by the architect Andrei Stakenschneider in the mid-nineteenth century. It is decorated with columns and pilasters of white marble; the upper landing is adorned by a malachite vase. The staircase gets its name from the fact that the rooms on the lower floor of the building were once used by the Council of State.

We now enter the series of rooms containing Italian Renaissance works of art (Halls 207-224).

Room of Italian Art of the 13th to Early 15th Century
Andrei Stakenschneider
1850s
Hall 207

Ugolino di Tedice
Cross with the Crucifixion
Circa 1270
Tempera on panel. 90 × 62 cm
▨ Hall 207

The cross bearing a depiction of the
Crucifixion is the oldest work of Italian
painting in the Hermitage. Relatively
small crosses of this sort were used
in religious processions or placed in
family chapels. They came to Italy from
Byzantium and became quite common
in the twelfth and thirteenth centuries.
This particular example is the only
authenticated work by Ugolino di Tedice,
a Pisan artist of the second half of
the thirteenth century. It entered the
Hermitage in 1926 from the Stroganov
Palace museum in Leningrad.

Simone Martini
Virgin Mary from an Annunciation
1340–42
Tempera and gold on panel
30.5 × 21.5 cm
Hall 207

The Virgin is one wing of a diptych. The second panel is in the National Gallery in Washington. It shows the Archangel Gabriel bringing Mary the news that she is to give birth to Christ. The artist, a major figure in the Sienese trecento, was a painter at the papal court in Avignon. His manner of painting gives preference to the Gothic style with its elegant forms, bright colours and fine bending lines. Martini's Virgin is an embodiment of the Gothic ideal of female beauty.

This work came into the Hermitage in 1911 from the St Petersburg collection of Count Stroganov.

Fra Beato Angelico (Fra Giovanni da
Fiesole)
Virgin and Child with Ss Dominic and
Thomas Aquinas
1414-30
Tempera fresco. 197 × 187 cm
Hall 209

This Early Renaissance painter
belonged to the Dominican Order of
monks and was famed for his paintings
and frescoes on religious themes. Fra
Angelico produced this work for the
Monastery of San Domenico in Fiesole.
The restrained colours and balanced
composition create a sense of peace
and harmony. In 1882 the fresco was
purchased in Florence from two artists,
Mazzanti and Conti.

Fra Filippo Lippi
The Vision of St Augustine
Late 1450s – early 1460s
Tempera and oil on panel
29 × 51.5 cm
▨ Hall 213

This painting by the outstanding Florentine artist is based on an episode from the story of the life of Saint Augustine, the Bishop of Hippo in North Africa. One day, while reflecting on the dogma of the Holy Trinity, Augustine saw an angel in the guise of a child spooning water from the sea. In response to the bishop's questions, the child-angel told him that it was as impossible for human reason to grasp the mystery of God's threefold nature as it was to drain the sea with a spoon. The artist may have been the first to tackle this subject. The action is set amongst the hills of Tuscany and a stream represents the sea. In the upper right-hand corner we can see one of the symbols of the Trinity – a three-face sun disk.

Originally this painting was in the lower part of an altar. It came into the museum in 1917 from the Princess of Oldenburg's Petrograd collection.

Filippino Lippi
The Adoration
Mid-1480s
Oil on copper, transferred from
panel. Diameter 53 cm
▨ Hall 213

Filippino Lippi, the son
of the artist Fra Filippo
Lippi, was a pupil of the
famous Sandro Botticelli.
Like his teacher, Filippino
Lippi gave preference to
elongated proportions and
exquisite forms. Against
the background of a Tuscan
landscape, Mary and the angels
worship the new-born Christ.
This Adoration is one of the first
paintings in Italian art in which
the landscape is in keeping with
the mood and appearance of the
personages. The work came into
the Hermitage in 1911 from the
St Petersburg collection of Count
Stroganov.

Perugino (Pietro Vannucci)
St Sebastian
Circa 1495
Tempera and oil on panel
53.5 × 39.5 cm
▨ Hall 213

According to legend
Sebastian, a captain of the
Praetorian Guard under Emperor
Diocletian, was sentenced to
death for his Christian faith.
The Emperor ordered his
soldiers to tie him to a post
and shoot arrows at him like
a target. Traditionally Italian
artists depicted the full figure
of Sebastian pierced by arrows,
but Perugino's painting shows
only the upper part of the young
man's figure and his beautiful
face lit up by prayer. The artist
wrote his own name in gold on
the arrow that runs through the
saint's neck.
    This painting entered the
museum in 1910 from the
Rome collection of Marchese
Campanari.

The Leonardo da Vinci Room
Andrei Stakenschneider, 1858

Leonardo da Vinci
Madonna and Child
(Benois Madonna;
Madonna with a Flower)
1478-80
Oil on canvas, transferred from
panel. 42 × 33 cm
▦ **Hall 214**

This is one of two early
Madonnas by Leonardo.
The British Museum and Uffizi
Gallery possess preparatory drawings and sketches for this painting
by the great master. The oil paints
that were replacing tempera
helped him to achieve the subtle
transitions of light and shade that
form the basis of the celebrated
sfumato technique. Leonardo
depicted the young mother with
clothing and a hairstyle in the
Florentine fashion of his own
day playing with her infant son
and holding out to him a crucifer
flower – a traditional symbol of
the Passion. For that reason the
Hermitage work is sometimes
known as the Madonna with a
Flower. The second name is due to
the fact that the painting entered
the Hermitage in 1914 from the
collection of Maria Benois.

Leonardo da Vinci
Madonna and Child
(Litta Madonna)
1490-91
Tempera on canvas,
transferred from panel
42 × 33 cm
▨ Hall 214

The second Madonna in the Hermitage collection was apparently painted in Milan, during Leonardo's time at the court of Lodovico Sforza. A silver-point preliminary drawing for it is now in the Louvre in Paris. The appearance of Mary has been transformed into an ideal image of the Virgin; the figure of the Christ-Child was modelled using extremely fine chiaroscuro (light and shade). The balanced composition and serene mountain landscape beyond the window reflect the Humanist concept of the harmony and grandeur of the universe. This work by Leonardo heralds the transition to a new style of painting - the High Renaissance. It entered the museum in 1865 from the collection of Count Litta in Milan, from whom it gets its second name.

Francesco Melzi
Flora
Circa 1520
Oil on canvas
Transferred from panel
76 × 63 cm
▓ Hall 215

Melzi was Leonardo da Vinci's favourite pupil who followed the master to France and remained with him to the end of his life.

The artist used a number of his great teacher's famous devices: soft sfumato, restrained colours, as well as the elegant pose and mysterious half-smile on the lips of the sitter. That is why until the 1850s this painting was attributed to Leonardo.

Who is depicted on the canvas is still a mystery. Some scholars believed that it is a portrait of a noble lady at the court of François I, others suggest that it is Mona Lisa.

According to Classical mythology Flora was the wife of west wind Zephyr, mother of all the plants. Melzi depicted Flora with aquilegia, symbol of fertility, in her hand.

This painting came into the museum in 1850 from the Hague collection of Wilhelm II.

Pontormo (Jacopo Carucci)
Madonna and Child with Saint
Joseph and John the Baptist
1520s
Oil on canvas. 120 × 98.5 cm
▓ Hall 216

Pontormo was an outstanding exponent of early Florentine Mannerism – a Late Renaissance tendency whose followers rejected the principle of harmony and began to seek their own artistic language.

Pontormo treats the traditional subject in a new way: the composition is deliberately disrupted by intersecting volumes and contrasting patches of colour. The red and green seem particularly bright alongside the pale pink face of the Virgin and body of the Christ-Child.

The Uffizi Gallery in Florence possesses a preliminary drawing for the Hermitage canvas and a copy of the painting can be found in the Royal Castle in Warsaw. The painting entered the Hermitage in 1923 from the collection of Countess Mordvinova.

Giulio Romano
Love Scene
1524-26
Oil on canvas. 163 × 337 cm
■ Hall 216

Giorgione
Judith
Early 1500s
Oil on canvas. 144 × 66.5 cm
■ Hall 217

Giulio Romano, one of Raphael's most gifted pupils, began with monumental murals transfused with an entirely Raphaelesque spirit and reminiscent of the works of his great teacher.

Soon, however, Romano freed himself of Raphael's influence and Renaissance ideals. His later independent work illustrates the Mannerist search for a new means of expression.

According to one version this Love Scene depicts the romance between Zeus and Alcmene that led to the birth of the great hero Hercules. It has been suggested that the painting is an allegorical allusion to the secret marriage of Federigo II Gonzaga and Isabella Boschetti.

This painting came into the museum no earlier than 1774 and was then known as A Gallant Scene.

From the Mannerism room (Hall 215) we turn around and return to the very first room of the Italian Renaissance (Hall 207). From there we move on to the display of Venetian art (Halls 217-223).

Judith, a masterpiece of Renaissance painting, was formerly attributed to Raphael. Today it has been definitively identified as a work by Giorgione, an artist who in many ways determined the course taken by Venetian painting in the sixteenth century. The apocryphal tale of Judith who saved her native city from an Assyrian invasion was often illustrated in the Renaissance era. Giorgione eschewed the tradition of depicting the actual moment when the heroine cut off the head of the enemy commander Holofernes after he fell asleep in his tent. Instead the artist created a lyrical image of Judith reflecting on the deed she has performed. The cool of the morning landscape and the enchanting figure of Judith convey an idea of the world as a harmonious whole, in which life and death are inextricably linked.

This painting once belonged to King Charles I of England. It came into the Hermitage in 1772 from the collection of Baron Crozat de Thiers in Paris. Between 1968 and 71 Judith underwent a restoration that brought out the wealth of nuances in the artist's painting.

Titian (Tiziano Vecellio)
The Repentant Mary Magdalene
1560
Oil on canvas. 118 × 97 cm
Hall 221

According to legend, after meeting
Christ the sinful Mary Magdalene
withdrew to the desert where she
mourned her previous sins. Titian
depicted Mary Magdalene several times
but the Hermitage version is justly
considered the best – the artist himself
did not part with the painting until the
end of his days. After the artist's death
his son sold his house together with
the painting to the patrician Cristoforo
Barbarigo. The canvas came into the
Hermitage in 1850.

Paolo Veronese
The Lamentation
Between 1576 and 82
Oil on canvas. 147 × 111.5 cm
▨ Hall 222

The Lamentation, one of the best works by Veronese, a great member of the Venetian school, was created for the Church of Santi Giovanni e Paolo in Venice.

After making his name with bright festive scenes, towards the end of his life the artist turned to tragic subjects. The figures depicted on the canvas are the Virgin Mary and an angel bend over the body of Christ. An x-ray study of the painting showed that a second angel supported the Saviour's body on the left, but was painted out by the artist. The dramatic effect is achieved by the contrast of warm and cold colours: the pink clothing of the angel, the gold of the hair and the cold hue of Christ's dead body.

This masterpiece was the pride of the collection of King Charles I of England. Later it came into the collection of Baron Crozat de Thiers in Paris, from where it entered the Hermitage in 1772.

The display of Venetian Renaissance art ends with the collection of applied art, the pride of which is the celebrated Venetian glass (Hall 223). From here we go through once more to the Mannerism room (Hall 215) and head for the Hermitage Theatre. We can only go as far as the foyer of the Hermitage Theatre (Hall 225).

The Hermitage Theatre. Foyer
■ Hall 225

The Raphael Loggias
1783-1792
■ Hall 227

The building of the Hermitage Theatre was constructed in 1783-89 by the Italian architect Giacomo Quarenghi on the corner of the Winter Canal and Neva embankment.

The foyer of the theatre was designed by Yury Velten in 1783, but decorated later by the celebrated Leonty Benois. The gallery that contains the foyer was finished in the Rococo style. The tall windows that fill the space with light go right down to the floor and provide superb views of the Neva and the Winter Canal. Famous Russian actors of the eighteenth and nineteenth centuries performed in the theatre. In January 1991 the restored Hermitage Theatre again opened its doors to visitors.

Coming out of the foyer and turning left we find ourselves in the famous Raphael Loggias gallery (Hall 226).

In the 1780s, on the orders of Empress Catherine II, Giacomo Quarenghi reproduced here the famous gallery in the Vatican Palace in Rome that was frescoed to designs by Raphael. The murals had as their subjects episodes from the Old and New Testaments and are therefore sometimes known as "Raphael's Bible". The decorative grotesques that separate the scenes appeared in the artist's work under the influence of murals discovered in the Golden House, Emperor Nero's palace in Rome. The copies of Raphael's frescoes were made for the Hermitage under the direction of Christoph Unterberger.

Just by the entrance to the Loggias is a door through which we reach the Raphael Hall (Hall 229) designed by Leo von Klenze which contains masterpieces of Italian majolica and two paintings by Raphael.

Raphael
Conestabile Madonna
1504
Tempera on canvas, transferred from
panel. 17.5 × 18 cm
▓ Hall 229

The Conestabile Madonna is one of
Raphael's earliest works, commissioned
by Duke Alfano di Diamante. The artist
created a unique image of the Virgin that
brought him enduring fame. Raphael's
Madonnas, devoid of features of ordinary
everydayness, yet at the same time
earthly and real, embodied the artist's
dream of an ideally beautiful human
being.

Alexander II acquired this tondo
(round painting) in 1870 from the Italian
Count Conestabile, whose name it bears.
During restoration in 1881 the painting
was transferred from wood to canvas. It
is conjectured that the gilded frame that
until 1881 formed a single whole with
the base of the painting was designed by

Raphael himself. The ornamental motifs
in the frame can also be found in the
Raphael Loggias (Hall 227).

**The Holy Family (Madonna with
the Beardless Joseph)**
1506
Tempera and oil on canvas, transferred
from panel. 72.5 × 57 cm
▓ Hall 229

The Hermitage's second Raphael was
bought by Catherine II in 1772 with the
aid of Denis Diderot and Prince Dmitry
Golitsyn from the heirs of Baron Crozat
de Thiers. The work dates from the
early, Florentine period in the artist's
career.

The subject is founded upon the
traditional depiction of Mary, the Infant
Jesus and Joseph that became common
in European art from the Renaissance
onwards. A sense of the spiritual
unity of the personages is achieved

through the planned organization of space, the skilful alternation of colours and the smoothness of the figures' outlines that form a compositional oval within the painting. The artist invested the personages with entirely realistic features: the Virgin's dress and hairstyle accord with Florentine fashion of the day, while Joseph, in defiance of established tradition, is depicted without a beard, for which reason the painting is sometimes called the Madonna with the Beardless Joseph.

Continuing to the end of the hall we find ourselves in the first of two Italian Skylight Halls (Halls 237 and 238).

The Italian Skylight Halls
▦ Halls 237-238

Because of the way they are lit from above, the grandest halls in the New Hermitage became known as the Skylight Halls. The Large and Small Italian Skylight Halls contain a display of Italian Baroque painting from the seventeenth and eighteenth centuries. The overhead lighting, the windowless walls covered with matte paint that does not reflect and the layout were all specifically designed for the

display of large-scale paintings. At the same time the architect, Leo von Klenze, decorated the Skylight Halls in emulation of sumptuous palatial halls. The interiors get an upbeat grandeur from the ornamental lacework of gilded stucco on the ceilings and decorative ensembles of unique works of Russian lapidary art from the nineteenth century – the large hall is adorned by items made from Urals malachite and porphyry, the small hall with Badashan lapis-lazuli and rhodonite.

Caravaggio
The Lute-Player
Circa 1595
Oil on canvas. 94 × 119 cm
▦ Hall 234

Caravaggio was the founder of genre painting and the still life in Italian painting. The Lute-Player, the only work in Russia by this master, was acquired in 1808 at the sale of the Giustiniani gallery collection in Rome in 1808. The canvas superbly illustrates the innovative features of Caravaggio's work: an interest in particular specific motifs, the material

beauty of objects and the conveying of form through sharp contrasts of light and shade.

The subject matter is not as simple as it seems at first glance. The book of music lying in front of the youth shows a part of Arcadelt's madrigal *You know that I love you*, while the cracked lute symbolizes unrequited love.

Caravaggio had no pupils, but his influence on European art was enormous: his method of working became the foundation for one of the key tendencies in late sixteenth- and early seventeenth-century art that is known as "Caravaggism".

Antonio Canale, nicknamed Canaletto, belonged to the school of Venetian artists who painted *vedute*, urban landscapes. This canvas gives a panoramic view of the most celebrated part of Venice: the Palace of the Doges, the Biblioteca Marciana and the church of Santa Maria della Salute. Smartly dressed Venetians are crowding on the embankment to greet the delegation of the French ambassador, Jacques Vincent Languet, Count of Gergy. The urban landscape produced by Canaletto is marked by topographical precision and a distinctive romantic interpretation. The glamour and colourfulness of the formal reception, the noise of the crowd, the abundance of light and air convey the unique charm of Venice. The canvas came into the museum between 1772 and 74.

Canaletto
The Reception of the French
Ambassador in Venice
1740s
Oil on canvas. 181 × 259.5 cm
■ Hall 238

Jacopo Tintoretto
The Nativity of John the Baptist
Circa 1550
Oil on canvas. 181 × 266 cm
██ Hall 237

This canvas was long believed to depict the Nativity of the Virgin Mary, while in actual fact it is devoted to an episode in the story of John the Baptist. The priest Zachariah, struck dumb by God for failing to believe the prophecy that he would have a son, recovered his voice after writing that, in accordance with the divine will, the boy's name was to be John.

Tintoretto treated the religious subject as a dynamic genre scene.

The canvas came into the museum in 1772 from the collection of Baron Crozat de Thiers.

SPANISH PAINTING
of the 16th and 17th centuries

FIRST
FLOOR

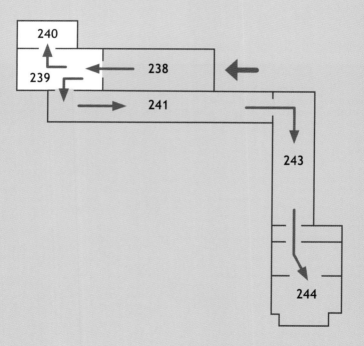

240

239

238

241

243

244

Spanish art is displayed in Halls 239 and 240

Luis de Morales
Virgin and Child with a Distaff
in the Form of a Cross
1570s
Oil on canvas, transferred from panel
71.5 × 52 cm
■ Hall 240

Luis de Morales was nicknamed El Divino – "the Divine". The central themes of his work were suffering and Christian sacrifice. In the treatment of the images one can sense the traditions of the Middle Ages that endured for a very long time in Spain.

The Virgin in the Hermitage painting is an embodiment of universal sorrow and tragedy. She looks at her son with boundless spiritual pain. The spindle and distaff in the form of a cross symbolize the agonizing death that lies in store for the Christ-Child.

The cold tone and smooth, enamel-like surface of the painting are characteristic of this artist. The painting came into the museum in 1846.

Juan Pantoja de la Cruz
Portrait of Don Diego de Villamayor
1605
Oil on canvas. 89 × 71 cm
■ Hall 240

The work of Pantoja de la Cruz laid the foundations for the Spanish aristocratic portrait. The artist worked at the court of Phillip II and Phillip III. He produced many formal depictions of Spanish grandees, in which he combined outward splendour with a strikingly truthful presentation of the appearance and character of the model.

The subject of the Hermitage canvas is shown in knightly armour in keeping with early seventeenth-century tradition. The heavy armour, painted by the artist down to the last details, invests the figure with significance and grandeur. Yet at the same time the youth decked out in

iron and lace bears little resemblance to a warrior. Beneath the bulky breastplate we sense the delicate, puny frame of an adolescent and the pallid face testifies to his sickliness.

The painting came into the museum in 1814 from the Amsterdam collection of the British banker William Coesvelt.

El Greco
The Apostles Peter and Paul
Between 1587 and 92
Oil on canvas. 121.5 × 105 cm
■ Hall 240

This is one of the first joint depictions in Spanish painting of the chief apostles of the Christian Church, Peter and Paul. The saints are depicted at the moment of the dispute in Antioch. This was an argument over whether Jewish Christians could share a meal with Gentiles. Before the coming of Jesus Christ sitting at the same table as non-Jews was considered an unworthy and defiling act. Jesus, though, ate with tax-collectors and sinners, thus showing that all the ancient prohibitions had lost their force and the Kingdom of Heaven was open to all. But it was no easy matter to lay aside the customs of one's ancestors. This became the heart of the dispute in which Paul rebuked Peter for lacking the boldness to go the whole way and share a communal meal with former pagans. The key theme of the painting is the clash of contradictory human characters. The contrast of the images is underlined by the composition, the colour scheme and the gestures of the pair: the humble, irresolute Peter (on the left) and the strong-willed, irreconcilable Paul (on the right).

The Hermitage canvas preceded the "apostolados" – a series of paintings devoted to the depiction of Christ and the twelve apostles. The canvas came into the museum in 1911.

Diego Velazquez
Luncheon
1617-1618
Oil on canvas. 108.5 × 102 cm
▨ **Hall 239**

The Hermitage's *Luncheon* dates from the early, Sevillian period in Velazquez's career, when the artist was fascinated with the depiction of genre scenes or *bodegones* – "tavern pieces".

Velzaquez produced lively expressive images of people engaged in their everyday affairs. Seeking as realistic a depiction as possible, the artist employed the device of contrasting lighting, in which the influence of Caravaggio is unarguably present. It has been suggested that in the youth

here Velzaquez depicted himself. To all appearances the other participants in the meal were also well known to the painter – their images recur in many of Velzaquez's canvases.

The painting has an allegorical subtext. We have here the three ages, the three aspects of human life. The personages are united by a morning meal consisting of fish, pomegranate, bread and wine – traditional symbols of Christ.

A variant of the Hermitage *Luncheon* is displayed in the Museum of Fine Arts in Budapest.

This work came into the Hermitage between 1763 and 74.

Francisco de Zurbaran
The Girlhood of the Virgin
Circa 1660
Oil on canvas. 73.5 × 53.5 cm
■ Hall 239

Francisco de Zurbaran made his name as the creator of large paintings for the monasteries of Seville and its hinterland. The artist turned his hand to the subject of the childhood of the Virgin several times. In the Hermitage painting created at the end of the artist's life Mary is shown at prayer. The dark neutral background and the almost complete absence of details force the viewer to devote particular attention to the child's face. Despite her age, the girl is serious and collected, her thoughts turned to God.

Alexander I bought this painting along with other masterpieces of Spanish painting in 1814 from the British banker William Coesvelt.

Bartolomé Esteban Murillo
Boy with a Dog
Between 1655 and 60
Oil on canvas. 70 × 60 cm
■ Hall 239

Bartolomeo Esteban Murillo, the last major Spanish painter of the seventeenth century, was the founder and first president of the Seville Academy and enjoyed great fame in his own lifetime. Murillo's paintings were in such demand that the king issued a decree banning their removal from the country.

Boy with a Dog is one of Murillo's finest genre compositions. The image of a street urchin delighted by the appearance of a dog is enchanting in its sincerity. The companion piece to the Hermitage painting – Girl with Fruit – is on display in the Pushkin Museum of Fine Arts in Moscow.

This work came into the Hermitage in 1772 from the Paris collection of the Duc de Choiseul.

From the Spanish Skylight Hall we enter the Gallery of the History of Ancient Painting (Hall 241).

The Gallery of the History of Ancient Painting
Hall 241

This gallery was conceived by Leo von Klenze with an educational intention – to remind visitors to the museum of the pre-history of European painting. Eighty paintings on subjects from Ancient Greek mythology decorate the walls of the hall. The artist Georg Hiltensperger produced them using the ancient encaustic technique – using wax-based paints on brass sheets.

The gallery is used to display works by the outstanding Neo-Classical sculptor Antonio Canova (1757-1822) and his followers. The Gallery of the History of Ancient Painting itself is evidence of how people viewed the Ancient World in the nineteenth century.

We pass along the gallery and come out in the Knights' Hall (Hall 243)

The Knights' Hall
Hall 243

This room of the New Hermitage originally housed the collection of old coins.

Today it contains an extremely rich collection of Western European arms and armour from the fifteenth to seventeenth centuries. The display presents the history of knightly armour, tournament, war and hunting equipment, as well as edged weapons and firearms.

From the Knights' Hall we move on to the Twelve-Column Hall (Hall 244).

The Twelve-Column Hall
Hall 244

This hall was intended for the numismatic collection and so the walls are embellished with relief portraits of famous medal-makers. The interior is decorated by grey granite columns, plaster sculpture and gilded ornamental motifs.

FIRST
FLOOR

FLEMISH AND DUTCH PAINTING
of the 17th centuries

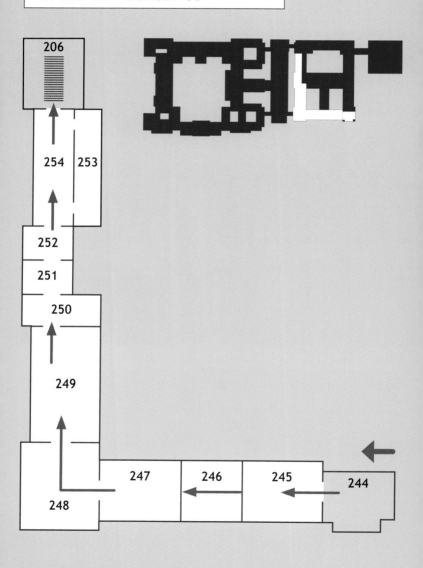

206

254 | 253

252

251

250

249

247 | 246 | 245 | 244

248

From the Twelve-Column Hall we turn right and come to the display of Flemish art (Halls 245-247).

Jacob Jordaens
The Bean King
Circa 1638
Oil on canvas. 157 × 211 cm
▨ **Hall 245**

The Bean King is a famous work by Jacob Jordaens, one of the greatest masters of the Flemish Baroque. The subject is inspired by the popular family festivities held each year in the Low Countries on 6 January – Epiphany or the Feast of the Magi. According to Christian legend that was the day when the Magi came to worship the infant Christ.

The painting shows a scene of wild celebration of the "king and queen" of the evening. By tradition on that day a pie was served with a bean baked into it. Whichever of the diners found the bean in their slice was declared "monarch" for the evening, chose a consort and appointed courtiers. The others were obliged to obey the whims of the new-found "monarch".

Many versions of this painting were produced earlier by Jordaens and still exist, but the Hermitage variant is justly

considered one of the best.

The painting was transferred to the Hermitage from Petrograd museum of the Academy of Arts in 1922.

Anthony van Dyck
Self-Portrait
Late 1620s – early 1630s
Oil on canvas. 116.5 × 93.5 cm
▦ Hall 246

Anthony van Dyck was one of the greatest masters of the formal portrait.

This self-portrait was painted when the artist was at the height of his powers. Van Dyck depicted himself youthful and elegant, in an exquisite silk camisole. The image is an embodiment of contemporary concepts of the artist as a man privy to the world of beauty and harmony.

This canvas was acquired in 1772 from the Paris collection of Baron Crozat de Thiers.

Peter Paul Rubens
**Portrait of a Maid of Honour to the
Infanta Isabella**
Mid-1620s
Oil on panel. 64 × 48 cm
░ Hall 247

This portrait is considered a
posthumous depiction of Rubens's
daughter, Clara Serena, who died in 1623
at the age of twelve. In this moving,
astonishingly tender depiction of a young
lady, Rubens set down the picture of his
daughter already grown-up that he had in
his mind's eye.

The title given to the portrait
was prompted by the inscription on
a preparatory drawing that is in the
Albertina collection in Vienna. It came
into the Hermitage in 1772 from the
collection of Baron Crozat de Thiers in
Paris.

Peter Paul Rubens
The Union of Earth and Water
Circa 1618
Oil on canvas. 222.5 × 180.5 cm
Hall 247

The full-blooded, joyful art of Rubens marked the highest flight of the Flemish school of painting. The picture is based on a mythological subject – the marriage between Cybele, the goddess of the earth, and the sea god Neptune. Probably Rubens also gave expression to his contemporaries' dream that the Dutch would lift their blockade from the mouth of the River Scheldt, giving Flanders back access to the sea. There is justification also for a wider interpretation: that we have here a glorification of union of two principles – earth and water, male and female, the foundations of earthly life, harmony and perpetual renewal. This work came into the Hermitage between 1798 and 1800.

Peter Paul Rubens
Bacchus
Between 1636 and 40
Oil on canvas, transferred from panel. 191 × 161.3 cm
Hall 247

Rubens turned his hand to the depiction of Bacchus, the ancient god of wine-making, on several occasions.

Rubens's Bacchus is far removed from ancient ideals. This feast attended by a satyr, a maenad and cupids is a sort of hymn to unbridled lack of restraint, the elemental, the earthly.

The Hermitage Bacchus, painted in the last years of the artist's life, was particularly dear to the artist. Rubens kept it in his studio right up to his death. It came into the Hermitage in 1772 from the collection of Baron Crozat de Thiers in Paris

From the Hall of Netherlandish Art (Hall 248) we turn right into the Tent-Roofed Hall (Hall 249) – the first in the section of Dutch painting (Halls 249-254).

Frans Hals
Portrait of a Young Man Holding a Glove
Circa 1650
Oil on canvas. 80 × 66.5 cm
▦ Hall 249

The Dutch portraitist Frans Hals rejected the formal schemata characteristic of portrait painting in previous eras. His images seem alive and unforced, as if they have been snatched from genre scenes. The well-groomed, self-confident Dutch burgher in the Hermitage canvas behaves naturally and simply. The "theatrical" turn of the figure, the gesture of the hands and the barely perceptible smile seem unpremeditated, accidental. They have been caught on the fly and instantly set down. The energetic, sweeping, seemingly casual brushstrokes and the dynamic line of the silhouette intensify still further the illusion of a fleeting moment.

This painting was among the group that came into the Hermitage in 1764 from the collection of the Berlin merchant Johann Ernst Gotzkowsky.

Frans Hals
Male Portrait
Before 1660
Oil on canvas. 84.5 × 67 cm
Hall 249

In this late work Hals's special
sense of colour manifested itself in full
measure. The artist attains striking
painterly effects using shades of black,
silvery grey and white. This work came
into the Hermitage between 1763 and 74.

Willem Claesz Heda
Breakfast with a Crab
1648
Oil on canvas. 118 × 118 cm
Hall 249

Looking at the Hermitage Breakfast it is easy to understand how the seventeenth-century Dutch came up with the term *stilleven* – "still life". The painting is transfused with a sense of domestic warmth and cosy sufficiency.

The unfinished glass of wine, the plate moved to the edge, the lemon, the crusty roll and the huge crab testify to the recent presence of the master of the house, to his tastes and habits.

The work of Willem Claesz Heda laid the foundations of a new subgenre of the still life that came to be known as "Breakfasts".

This work was added to the Hermitage collection in 1920.

As he also managed the family tavern, Jan Steen frequently witnessed noisy merrymaking and celebrations. The artist quite often depicted episodes of "idle" existence in his work. In the Hermitage canvas Steen is believed to have depicted himself and his wife Margaretha in the role of carefree revellers. The artist treated the scene of the end of a drunken evening with his inherent subtle, good-natured humour, without sanctimonious precepts and moralizing. The particular charm of this painting lies also in the virtuoso way in which Steen depicted the texture of fabrics and articles in the room. The canvas came into the museum in 1764.

Jan Steen
The Revellers
Circa 1660
Oil on panel. 39 × 30 cm
Hall 249

Rembrandt
Flora
1634
Oil on canvas. 125 × 101 cm
▊ **Hall 254**

The Hermitage boasts a magnificent collection of paintings and graphic works by the great Dutch artist, Rembrandt van Rijn (1606-69).

This painting was executed soon after the artist's marriage. Rembrandt depicted his young wife, Saskia van Uylenburgh in the guise of the Roman goddess of spring and flowers. The girl is wearing a wreath

and holding a thyrsus (staff) – both attributes of Flora. The artist devoted great attention to conveying the rich eastern clothing that glistens with the play of precious embroidery. In this period Rembrandt collected antiques and oriental fabrics and they often featured in his paintings.

The artist presents the image of his young wife with unconcealed love and reverence. Rembrandt depicted his dear Saskia as Flora twice more, in 1635 and 1641, and he always painted her likeness with a special awe and tenderness. This canvas was acquired between 1770 and 74.

Rembrandt
Danae
1636
Oil on canvas. 185 × 202.5 cm
▨ **Hall 254**

In contrast to Titian, who depicted the actual encounter between Danae and Zeus, Rembrandt recorded the moment preceding the lovers' assignation. This deviation from established practice enabled the artist to reveal the complex gamut of the heroine's feelings: her excitement, awe, embarrassment and simultaneous joy and amazement at the stream of golden light that heralds the approach of Zeus.

We know that originally Danae's face resembled Saskia, the artist's first wife. When he repainted the work in 1649, Rembrandt made the personage more mature, giving her the features of his second wife, Hendrickje Stoffels.

This painting was in restoration for more than ten years after a terrible act of vandalism was committed upon it in 1985.

The canvas came into the museum in 1772 from the Paris collection of Baron Crozat de Thiers.

Rembrandt
The Sacrifice of Isaac
1635
Oil on canvas. 193 × 132 cm
Hall 254

According to the Book of Genesis, God tested Abraham's obedience by demanding that he sacrifice his only son, Isaac. At the very moment when Abraham raised his hand to strike the youth and angel appeared and restrained the obedient patriarch.

In tackling this Old Testament episode the artist created a scene full of drama and psychological tension.

This canvas was acquired in 1779 as part of the Houghton Hall collection of the late Sir Robert Walpole.

Rembrandt
The Holy Family
1645
Oil on canvas. 117 × 91 cm
▨ **Hall 254**

We have here a scene in the house of Joseph the carpenter. Mary looks with reverent care at the face of the sleeping child, while the head of the family is busy at his craft.

Rembrandt has treated the religious subject as a genre scene: maternal love that brings warmth to human existence,

the charm of quiet family life. Only the mystic divine light penetrating into the room and the hosts of angels indicate that we are looking not simply at a humble Dutchwoman, but at the Virgin with the infant Christ.

Mary's facial features resemble Hendrickje Stoffels. Hendrickje came into Rembrandt's life in the role of an ordinary servant, but soon became the artist's second wife.

This painting was acquired by Catherine II in 1772 from the collection of Baron Crozat de Thiers.

Rembrandt
Portrait of an Old Man in Red
First half of the 1650s
Oil on canvas. 108 × 86 cm
▨ Hall 254

The depiction of the "Old Man in Red" relates to the famous series of old men and women that Rembrandt painted chiefly in the later years of his life.

This portrait is a biography, an image in which line and colour reflect a whole human life. It was acquired in 1769.

Rembrandt
The Return of the Prodigal Son
Mid-1660s
Oil on canvas. 262 × 205 cm
▨ Hall 254

The subject of this painting is taken from the Gospel parable of the youth who requested his share of the inheritance from his father, left the family home and spent years leading a life of dissolution. After spending his whole fortune he returned, sick and ragged, to his father with a repentant heart. The father joyfully received the son whose return he had waited so long for. (Luke 15:20-24).

Rembrandt treated the scene of the meeting between father and repentant son as a tremendous human drama: the old man almost blinded by sorrow and the son who has known all the miseries of a wandering existence.

The scene is devoid of outward action and diversion. In the deep complex space Rembrandt singles out what is most important - the face of the old man, his hands

and the figure of the son. Standing in front of the painting, viewers find themselves part of the same circle of onlookers as those in the picture.

This work, painted shortly before the artist's death, is quite often called Rembrandt's testament: a summons to mercy, spiritual awakening and humanity.

The painting was transferred to the Hermitage in 1882 from the collection of Peter I kept in Monplaisir palace in Peterhof.

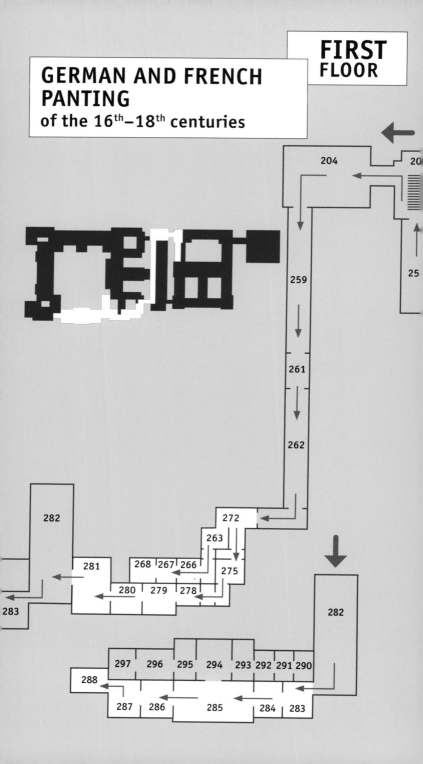

GERMAN AND FRENCH PANTING
of the 16ᵗʰ–18ᵗʰ centuries

204

20

259

25

261

262

282

272

263

281

268 267 266

275

280 279 278

283

282

297 296 295 294 293 292 291 290

288

287 286 285 284 283

Leaving the Rembrandt Hall we find ourselves back on the upper landing of the Council Staircase (Hall 206).

We need to return to the Winter Palace to continue our walk around the rooms and view the masterpieces of German and French painting. From the landing of the Council Staircase we turn left into the Pavilion Hall (Hall 204). From there we again walk along the gallery of mediaeval applied art and Netherlandish painting (Halls 259-262). Turning right at the end, in Hall 258, we make for the halls of the Winter Palace.

IF YOU WANT TO SEE

Traditionally German art is displayed in Halls 263-268. Unfortunately for technical reasons the display is often relocated. Ask the museum attendants to help you find the way to the display if you wish to view the masterpieces of this school of art.

Lucas Cranach the Elder
Venus and Cupid
1509
Oil on canvas, transferred from panel. 213 × 102 cm
Hall 264

Cranach was one of the greatest masters of the Northern Renaissance. His work blends the traditions of the Italian Renaissance and the strict religious morality of the Reformation period. The graceful goddess of love and beauty in the Hermitage variant of his beloved composition Venus and Cupid is at one and the same time the embodiment of beauty and a symbol of sin. While drawing viewers' attention to the goddess's voluptuous curves, Cranach places at the top of the painting a Latin inscription: "Reject Cupid's lasciviousness with all your might, or else Venus will possess your blinded soul." The Hermitage Venus was Cranach's first work on a classical subject and the first depiction of a nude goddess in the Northern Renaissance. The painting entered the Hermitage in 1769.

Lucas Cranach the Elder
The Virgin and Child
under the Apple-Tree
Circa 1530
Oil on canvas, transferred from panel.
87 × 59 cm
▮ Hall 264

This painting dates from the artists mature period. Its symbolic content is connected with the Christian dogma of the Fall and Salvation of the human race: the Christ-Child is holding an apple and bread – symbols of original sin and its redemption. Mary herself in the present context is a second Eve, redeeming the sin of the first ancestress.

While retaining a link with the devices of Gothic art, the painter produced what is already a Renaissance work. Sitting beneath the apple-tree, Cranach's Virgin is reminiscent of a refined society lady. The enchantingly beautiful landscape and the rich bright colours intensify the sense of the joyous perception of the real earthly world. The painting came into the Hermitage in 1851.

Ambrosius Holbein
Portrait of a Young Man
1518
Oil on panel. 44 × 32,5 cm
▮ Hall 264

This is a unique example of portrait painting by Ambrosius Holbein. For many years the painting was attributed to the famous Hans Holbein the Younger, Ambrosius's brother. Today there is no doubt as to who created the portrait.

Following the established traditions of the High Renaissance, the artist depicted the model close-up in a three-quarter turn against the background of an architectural landscape. The achievements of the Italian Renaissance adopted by Holbein are combined in this work with an attention to small details characteristic of German art.

The inscription in the cartouche gives the age of the subject – twenty – and the date when the work was painted - 1518. The monogram on the young man's beret has still not been deciphered. The painting entered the Hermitage between 1774 and 83.

Anton Raphael Mengs
Perseus and Andromeda
1777
Oil on canvas. 227 × 153.5 cm
▨ Hall 268

A personal advisor to Catherine II on matters of art, Anton Raphael Mengs was an acknowledged master of eighteenth-century Neo-Classicism. In his work this artist combined the ancient canons of beauty with the achievements of the Italian Renaissance.

The canvas was painted on motifs from the ancient myth of Perseus and

Andromeda: Andromeda, the daughter of King Cepheus, was left chained to a rock on the seashore as a sacrifice to a sea monster. Perseus defeated the monster, saved the girl and she became his bride.

The composition was borrowed from an ancient cameo, now in the Hermitage collection, that at one time belonged to Mengs's wife. The figure of Perseus is derived from the famous statue of the Apollo Belvedere, but the prototype for Andromeda was an ancient bas-relief in the Villa Doria Pamphili in Rome. The painting came into the Hermitage in 1780

Turning left from Hall 272 we enter the display of French art. We begin our acquaintance with it in Hall 273 and continue as far as Hall 281.

Corneille de Lyon
Female Portrait
Mid-1530s
Oil on panel. 20 × 15.5 cm
▪ Hall 273

Corneille de Lyon was famed chiefly as a master of the aristocratic portrait. The name of the woman depicted in the Hermitage painting is unknown, but the clothing and jewellery, painted by the artist almost in the technique of miniatures, and also the noble bearing leave little doubt that we are looking at a lady of high birth. Realistic reproduction of the model's appearance, something typical of sixteenth-century French art, is combined in this work with exquisite lines.

The painting entered the Hermitage in 1925 from the Shuvalov House museum in Leningrad.

Jacques Bellange
The Lamentation
1615-1617
Oil on canvas. 115 × 175 cm
▪ Hall 273

Today Bellange's work is recognized as one of the most enigmatic phenomena in European culture around the turn of the seventeenth century and the Hermitage canvas as a unique masterpiece of French Mannerism.

The guttering flame of the candle that fills the painting with an unreal light, the mysterious figures of the mourners whose attire is a strange mixture of historical dress and contemporary seventeenth-century fashion, and the blue-black colour scheme endow the religious scene with the character of a mystic rite.

This canvas was purchased from A. Leinberg in Tallinn in 1967.

Louis Le Nain
The Milkmaid's Family
1640-e
Oil on canvas. 51 × 59 cm
Hall 276

Le Nain was an exponent of the realistic tendency and founder of the "peasant genre" in French art in the first half of the seventeenth century. *The Milkmaid's Family*, painted when Le Nain was in his prime, gives us the best idea of this artist's manner of work. The old milkmaid, peasant and children standing around the donkey that feeds the family are united not by gestures or looks, but by the burdens and adversities of life. Through the low horizon and the placement of the figures on a hummock the artist invests the images of his lowly personages with monumentality. This canvas came into the Hermitage between 1774 and 83.

Nicolas Poussin
The Battle of the Israelites and Amalekites
Circa 1625
Oil on canvas. 97.5 × 134 cm
▨ Hall 279

The oeuvre of Poussin, the founding-father of Neo-Classicism in French painting, embodied the triumph of the rational principle: order and harmony. In search of inspiration the artist looked to the legacy of the Ancient World and the work of Italian Renaissance masters.

The Battle of the Israelites and Amalekites was the first painting that the artist produced in Italy, where he would spend the greater part of his working life, and his first depiction of an episode from the story of Moses. Moses watched the battle from the top of a hill and prayed for Joshua's victory. When he raised his arms to the heavens, the Israelites had the upper hand, but when he lowered them the tide turned in favour of the enemy. When his arms grew tired, Aaron and Hur supported them and so the Israelites defeated their foes.

The companion piece to the Hermitage painting – The Battle of the Israelites and Amorites – can be seen in the Pushkin Museum of Fine Arts in Moscow. This work came into the Hermitage between 1763 and 74.

Nicolas Poussin
Landscape with Polyphemus
1649
Oil on canvas. 150 × 199 cm
▨ **Hall 279**

Giving expression to the idea
of the all-embracing grandeur
of nature, Poussin created what
became known as "the heroic
landscape", which he enlivened
with mythological personages.
The Cyclops Polyphemus was
deeply in love with the sea
nymph Galatea, who preferred
the young shepherd Acis. The
one-eyed giant's passion finds
expression in the enchanting
sounds of the pipes that are
heard by mountains and valleys,
gods and humans. Poussin's pri-
maevally powerful, epic nature is
idealized: it is eternal, as eternal
as myths and love.

The mathematical exactitude
of the composition, the precise
organization of space and the
clarity of the artistic devices
accord with the Neo-Classicist's
conceptions of beauty and harmony in art. This work came into
the Hermitage in 1772.

We make a stop in the Alexander Hall (Hall 282).

The Alexander Hall
Alexander Briullov, 1839
▢ Hall 282

The decoration of this hall is dedicated to the memory of Emperor Alexander I and the "Patriotic War" of 1812.

The frieze that extends across the long walls incorporates enlarged copies of medals by the sculptor Fyodor Tolstoy that depicted in allegorical form the most significant events in the repulsion of Napoleon's invasion in 1812 and the subsequent foreign campaigns of 1813-14. A special place among these images is taken by a relief profile of Alexander I in the guise of the Slavonic hero Rodomysl contained in the lunette of the end wall. The medallions alternate with images of Victoria, the goddess of victory. The hall is further adorned with stucco decoration on the themes of military heroism.

We continue our walk through the display of French painting.

Antoine Watteau
An Embarrassing Proposal
Circa 1716
Oil on canvas. 65 × 84.5 cm
■ Hall 284

In Watteau's work almost all the genres and moods known to early 18th century painting are intertwined, but the artist has gone down in the history of art chiefly as a master of fêtes galantes – little scenes of the carefree, elegant life of the upper classes.

Exquisite ladies and gentlemen are relaxing in the bosom of nature. They talk, laugh, flirt and play-act without any regard for the viewer. The artist had depicted the special world of the Rococo era in which fantasy and reality are mixed up, in which there is neither action nor event, but only the barely detectable nuances of moods and emotions.

Colour and light in the painting have lost definition and thus intensify the sense of the ambiguity and uncertainty of what is taking place.

This work came into the Hermitage in 1769 from the Dresden collection of Count Brühl.

Antoine Watteau
The Capricious Woman
Circa 1718
Oil on canvas. 42 × 34 cm
▨ Hall 284

In a picturesque corner of an old
park a young, smartly dressed lady and a
gentleman are engaged in the customary
game of courtship. The girl's overt indif-
ference, her stubbornly pursed lips and
the gesture of her hand, irritably gather-
ing up her skirt, only amuse the suitor,
who has no intention of abandoning his
efforts.

Watteau has treated this fairly com-
monplace scene from society life with
gentle irony and lyricism, introducing a
barely detectable note of sadness and
dreaminess into his presentation.

This painting was transferred to the
Hermitage in 1923 from the Stroganov
Palace museum in Petrograd.

François Lemoine
Female Bather
Mid-1720s
Oil on canvas. 138 × 106.5 cm
▓ **Hall 285**

Thanks to his talent and influential patrons, François Lemoine forged a brilliant career at the court of Louis XV: in 1733 the artist became a professor of the Paris Academy and in 1736 he was awarded the title of First Painter to the King.

Lemoine was famed as the creator of large decorative murals in the halls of Versailles and in churches. He produced numerous canvases on mythological subjects, and the Hermitage's *Female Bather* belongs among these. The painting is a superb illustration of the refined and somewhat mannered style of an artist considered one of the founders of Rococo art.

Female Bather was purchased in Paris in 1771.

François Boucher
Landscape in the Environs of Beauvais
Early 1740s
Oil on canvas
49 × 58 cm
▓ **Hall 285**

Reflecting the tastes of his eminent clients, François Boucher chose for his landscapes modest rural motifs: watermills, squalid hovels, ponds and shady backwaters. The fascination with pastoral scenes was bound up with the theory, widely accepted among the French aristocracy, that only a person living in the bosom of nature, far from the bustle of the city, could be truly happy.

This painting has been in the Hermitage since 1923.

Jean Baptiste Siméon Chardin
Still Life with Attributes of the Arts
1766
Oil on canvas. 112 × 140.5 cm
Hall 287

This still life was painted for the St Petersburg Academy of Arts to a commission from Catherine II. Chardin was an unsurpassed master of texture and a superb colourist. Under this artist's brush ordinary objects acquire a special significance and greatness. It is an allegorical representation of the arts: the palette and paint-box stand for painting, the roll of technical drawings and set of drawing instruments architecture, the red morocco-leather case for papers drawing and, finally, sculpture is represented by a small statuette of *Mercury Tying His Sandal* by Jean Baptiste Pigalle. Depicted on the left is the cross of the Order of St Michael, the highest decoration awarded to the artist.

The still life pleased Catherine so much that she kept it in her private apartments. It came into the Hermitage in 1766.

Jean Honoré Fragonard
A Stolen Kiss
1780s
Oil on canvas. 45 × 55 cm
▨ Hall 288

It is said that this painting reminded its first owner, the Polish king Stanislaw Poniatowski of his affair with the future Empress Catherine II. This piquant, intimate scene by Frago, as the artist was fondly known in Paris, accords with the spirit of the late Rococo. The light, flowing outlines of the shapes and dashing smoothness of the brushstrokes combine here with a particular attention to texture: the artist conveyed with especial care the furnishings, rich clothing, gleaming with the delicate play of silk, the light wrap, patterned lace and ribbons.

This canvas belonged to the "Kiss Series" as, evidently, did a lost companion piece entitled *The Marriage Contract* that is now known only from an engraving. This work entered the Hermitage in 1895.

FIRST
FLOOR

ENGLISH PAINTING
of the 18th century
GRAND HALLS OF THE
WINTER PALACE

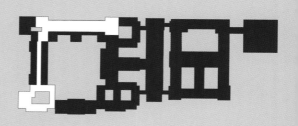

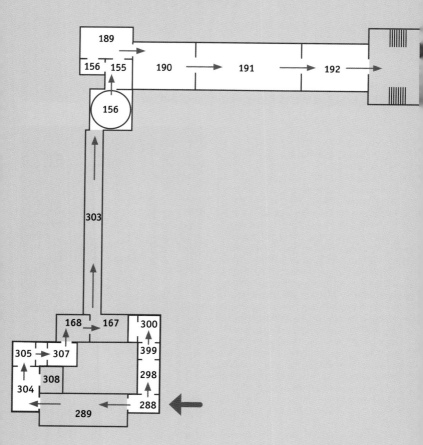

On the right in Halls 298-301 is the display of English painting. If you are not too tired we recommend visiting it. The display is arranged in such a way that we go round and come back to Hall 288. If you are nearly worn out or the halls are closed for the daily break (from 12 to 1), then we suggest carrying on to the White Hall (Hall 289), completing your introduction to the French art and heading for the Main Staircase by way of the sumptuous palace interiors.

IF YOU WANT TO SEE

If you have chosen to follow the shorter route and not visit the halls of English art then you can skip the next pages of the guide and resume on page 85.
Turning right from Hall 288 we enter the display of English art.

Thomas Gainsborough
Portrait of a Lady in Blue
Late 1770s
Oil on canvas. 76 × 64 cm
Hall 298

This is the only work in the Hermitage by Gainsborough, a master of the formal portrait and favourite artist of society ladies. Avoiding the conventionalities of the formal portrait, Gainsborough invested the image with true vitality. The relaxed pose, unforced gesture of the hand, slightly open lips and dreamy gaze allow us to form a real impression of the sitter. The refined harmony of cold hues - light and dark blues and silvers, the light, rapid translucent strokes applied with a small brush and virtuoso skill, and the abundance of half-tones invest this image with a special poetry and refinement. The painting entered the Hermitage between 1912 and 16.

Joshua Reynolds
Cupid Untying the Girdle of Venus
1788
Oil on canvas. 127.5 × 101 cm
Hall 300

This is a repetition of Reynolds's painting *The Snake in the Grass* that is now displayed in the Tate Gallery in London. The artist produced the Hermitage variant to a commission from Lord Carysfort. In 1792 the painting came into the Hermitage, where it acquired its present name. It has been suggested that the model for Venus was Emma Hart, better known as Lady Hamilton, the mistress of Admiral Nelson.

A warm Titianesque colour scheme, Flemish sensuality and a Rembrandtesque use of light and shade combine in this painting with an almost Rococo treatment of the subject. This work came into the Hermitage in 1792.

From Hall 167 we turn left and return by way of the display of English applied art to Hall 288.
We enter the White Hall (Hall 289) and complete our viewing of the French art.

The White Hall
Alexander Briullov, 1838-41
■ Hall 289

The architect Alexander Briullov created the elegant décor of the White Hall for the wedding of the heir to the Russian throne, the future Emperor Alexander II, and Princess Maximilienne Wilhelmine Marie of Hesse-Darmstadt, who took the name Maria Alexandrovna on her conversion to the Orthodox faith. The hall has come down to us unaltered since that time.

Architecturally the White Hall is reminiscent of rooms in Roman palaces. Arches on protruding pillars visually divide the space into three parts. The central section is most sumptuously decorated: rising above the Corinthian columns are four allegorical figures representing the arts; between the columns opposite the window is a magnificent fireplace made of coloured marbles and jasper.

Hubert Robert
The Ancient Temple known as "La Maison Carrée" at Nîmes
1783
Oil on canvas. 103 × 143 cm
▓ Hall 289

   This painting is an example of what is known as the "ruin genre" in French landscape painting. Ruins were exceptionally popular with a certain circle of the European public. Thanks to his great decorative talent Hubert Robert quite quickly attained fame and success. His grand architectural fantasies were a regular adornment of elegant salons and palaces. Robert's paintings were especially appreciated in Russia. His clients here included Catherine II, Paul I and Alexander I, members of the Russian aristocracy and major art patrons.
   Robert's art had a great influence on the evolution of Romanticism.
   This particular painting came into the Hermitage in 1933 from the State Museum Fund.

We leave the White Hall (Hall 289) and continue our acquaintance with the palace interiors.
First on our way is the luxurious Golden Drawing-Room (Hall 304).

The Gold Drawing-Room
Hall 304

This was the state drawing-room of Empress Maria Alexandrovna, the wife of Alexander II. Originally the room as decorated to Alexander Briullov's project in the 1830s had a different appearance: the walls were finished with white plaster and embellished with light gilded ornament. In the 1840s the interior was refurbished by

Andrei Stakenschneider, but it acquired its present appearance in the 1860s. It was then that, in accordance with the concept of the architect Vladimir Schreiber, the walls, doors and moulded ornament were all covered with fine gold leaf, which gave the drawing-room its name.

The sumptuous interior is enhanced by a splendid marble fireplace and a parquet floor made of precious varieties of wood.

The Crimson Cabinet
◼ Hall 305

This drawing-room adjoined Maria Alexandrovna's private apartments: here the Empress would read, hold musical soirées and meet her children. It was also the place where she kept her finest paintings – now gems of the Hermitage collection – Raphael's *Conestabile Madonna* and Murillo's *Immaculate Conception*.

When created in the 1830s by the architect Alexander Briullov, the room had a vaulted ceiling decorated with paintings. In the 1860s it was reconstructed by Harald Bosse under the guidance of his fellow architect Stakenschneider.

The walls of the drawing-room are lined with crimson silk woven with a pattern of notes and musical instruments. The fabric suffered badly during the Second World War and was recreated on the basis of authentic nineteenth-century samples.

The Boudoir
Harald Bosse, 1853
◼ Hall 306

The Boudoir in Empress Maria Alexandrovna's private apartments was decorated in the "Second Rococo" style by the architect Harald Bosse in the mid-nineteenth century. Bright red silk wall lining in combination with mirrors, gilding, painted insets and a ceiling painting creates a sense of luxury and refinement.

We pass through the Blue Bedroom (Hall 307), Hall 168 and from Hall 167 turn left to enter a corridor where tapestries are displayed (Hall 303). Following the corridor to the end we reach the Rotunda (Hall 156) and then the Large Moorish Dining-Room (Hall 155).

The Rotunda
Auguste Montferrand, 1830
Restored after the 1837 fire by Alexander Briullov
▨ Hall 156

The round hall created by Montferrand in 1830 linked the northern and western wings of the Winter Palace. After the fire of 1837 the interior was recreated by Alexander Briullov, who made minor changes to the original concept. The composition of the hall derives from the Roman Pantheon. The side niches of the Rotunda are decorated with fluted Corinthian columns.

At present the Rotunda is one of the display halls of the Department of Russian Culture relating to the time of Peter the Great.

The Large Moorish Dining-Room
Vasily Stasov, 1826
◼ Hall 155

This hall was created in 1826 to the design of the architect Vasily Stasov and later refurbished by Auguste Montferrand. After the 1837 fire it was restored by Alexander Briullov as the Large Dining-Room. Its design was inspired by elements of ancient architecture.

The Large Dining-Room got its second name from palace servants from Ethiopia (known as "Moors" in the eighteenth and nineteenth centuries) who guarded its entrance during receptions.

From the Large Moorish Dining-Room through the left-hand door we enter the Small Dining-Room (Hall 188).

The Small (White) Dining-Room
Alexander Krasovsky, 1894-95
◼ Hall 188

The Small Dining-Room was part of the apartments used by Nicholas II and his family. This small room became the setting for an act of revolutionary drama: in the small hours of 26 October 1917, Bolshevik supporters burst into the room and arrested the ministers of the Provisional Government. A memorial plaque on the mantelpiece records this event.

By way of the Small Dining-Room
(Hall 188) we reach the famous
Malachite Room (Hall 189).

The Malachite Room
Alexander Briullov, 1839
▨ Hall 189

The many-sided artistic potential of
the green mineral malachite are revealed
in the famous Malachite Room.

The architectural design and original
décor of this state drawing-room belong-
ing to Empress Alexandra Fiodorovna, the
wife of Nicholas I, were formed in 1839
by the architect Alexander Briullov. The
columns, pilasters, torcheres, fireplaces,
tables and a number of other items were
faced with malachite using the expensive
and laborious technique known as "Russian mosaic" to imitate a solid piece of
stone. The particular pride of the hall
is the malachite vase standing beneath
a gilded canopy. It adorned one of the
rooms of the palace even before the 1837
fire. The sense of sumptuous luxury that
prevails in the room is due to contrasts
of colour: the rich deep green of the
malachite, the abundant gilding and the
intense crimson tone of the drapery and
upholstery. The Malachite Room is interesting not just as a work of lapidary art,
but also as a place of history. Between
July and October 1917 the Provisional
Government headed by Alexander Keren-
sky held its meetings here.

From the Malachite Rooms we enter the halls that make up the Neva Enfilade of state rooms (Halls 190-192).

The Concert Hall
Vasily Stasov, 1830s
■ Hall 190

This hall was recreated in the Neo-Classical style after the 1837 fire by the architect Vasily Stasov. It now contains the silver tomb commissioned by Empress Elizabeth in the mid-eighteenth century to house the relics of St Alexander Nevsky.

The Nicholas Hall
Vasily Stasov, 1830s
▦ Hall 191

Stasov created this hall in place of the grand Ballroom that perished in the 1837 fire. After the death of Nicholas I a portrait of him was installed here and so the hall came to bear his name. This is the main hall of the suite of state rooms running along the Neva. It has a floor area of 1,103 square metres and was intended for official ceremonies and balls. Today it is used to house temporary exhibitions.

Through the Forehall (Hall 192) we come back to the landing of the Main Staircase from where we began our acquaintance with the Hermitage. We hope that this brief walk has aroused your interest in the treasures of the famous museum.

> Chose one of our thematic routes in the
> HERMITAGE IN 1 HOUR series and continue
> getting to know the Hermitage.

INDEX
OF STATE ROOMS

Luigi Premazzi
View of the New Hermitage from Millionnaya Street. 1861
Watercolour
32 x 46 cm

INDEX OF ARTISTS

The Hermitage in 1 Hour

State Rooms
Masterpieces
of Western European Painting:
14th – 18th Centuries

Text by Oleg Neverov

Editors: Polina Yermakova, Nina Zhutovsky

Editorial assistant: Catherine Okorokova

Editorial Director: Elena Krutova

Translated from the Russian by Paul Williams

Designed by David Plaksin

Photography:
Yuri Molodkovets, Leonard Heifetz,
Vladimir Terebenin, Valery Zubarov

ISBN 978-5-91208-134-7